MADDY & ME

Sue Overton Haringa

Balboa Press books may be ordered through booksellers or by contacting:

Balboa Press
A Division of Hay House
1663 Liberty Drive
Bloomington, IN 47403
www.balboapress.com
844-682-1282

Because of the dynamic nature of the Internet, any web addresses or links contained in this book may have changed since publication and may no longer be valid. The views expressed in this work are solely those of the author and do not necessarily reflect the views of the publisher, and the publisher hereby disclaims any responsibility for them.

ISBN: 978-1-9822-7941-7 (sc)
ISBN: 978-1-9822-7942-4 (hc)
ISBN: 978-1-9822-7943-1 (e)

Library of Congress Control Number: 2022902095

Print information available on the last page.

Balboa Press rev. date: 02/15/2022

BALBOA.PRESS
A DIVISION OF HAY HOUSE

MADDY & ME

A voyage I never thought I would take

Sue Overton Haringa

Hum, drum drum. The sound that wakes me. I'm asleep on the engine of my person, Wayne's truck in Echuca, Australia.

Today sounds different. Instead of silence and the soft bleating of sheep in the distance, there's this Hum, drum drum, I jump down off the engine onto the ground, but it's not grass, it's something hard like wood or metal. It's cold and the wind is strong. I'm drawn to a ledge. When I jump onto it all I can see is water all around me. It's like I'm in the middle of a big lake but I can see no land.

I'm hungry and smell food. I go down some stairs where a white haired dude with a long white beard is cooking something wonderful. He sees me; "Hey little guy, where did you come from?" He pets and makes over me for a while then feeds me bacon and something wonderful, soft and yellow which he called eggs.

My belly full, I make my way back to Maddy, my truck. I don't know why he called her that but it had been my home for a long time. I make my way up through the engine compartment into the back seat where my bed awaits. The ultra-vinyl warmed nicely from my body heat engulfs me in comfort and sleep.

Squeeks, scratching. I see rats all over the windshield trying to get in. Suddenly, a really big rat comes and scoots all the little rats away. He had beatty little rat eyes but they were kind. Then he was gone. I never saw any of the smaller rats again, but the big one came by daily to check on me. I called him King Arthur.

Life went on like this for so long I became used to being in the middle of a lake. I didn't know where I was but I had the shelter of Maddy, food and my friend, King Arthur.

One day I awake to many different sounds. Horns blowing, engines running and much other noise. Such confusion. Suddenly, Maddy and I were lifted into the air by a big hook. I was terrified! Maddy was put on a truck and it was moving along. I got the courage to look out the window and the ground was moving past so fast. It was a blur.

This went on for quite some time and suddenly Maddy was not moving. I hid underneath the seat and shivered in fear.

I awoke some time later and crept down through the engine compartment and onto the ground. I was on green grass again... The sound of hum, drum had stopped and all I could hear was the whisper of soft rain. I thought I was back in Echuca, so I crawled up into the backseat of Maddy and went fast asleep.

The next time I awake there are two people. They found me in the backseat and loved on me and called me Yota... I had only been called kitty before then so I finally had a name. The people were Jesse and Jenn and they were going to be my people.

Come to find out, Jesse had imported Maddy, a 1982 Toyota Hilux all the way from Australia to Seattle. This was an 8, 200mile journey by barge across the Pacific Ocean. The trip had taken nearly 10 weeks.

I live in Arlington, Washington with my new people Jesse and Jenn and their dogs Maizy and Porter.

And that's how I came to be an American cat named Yota.

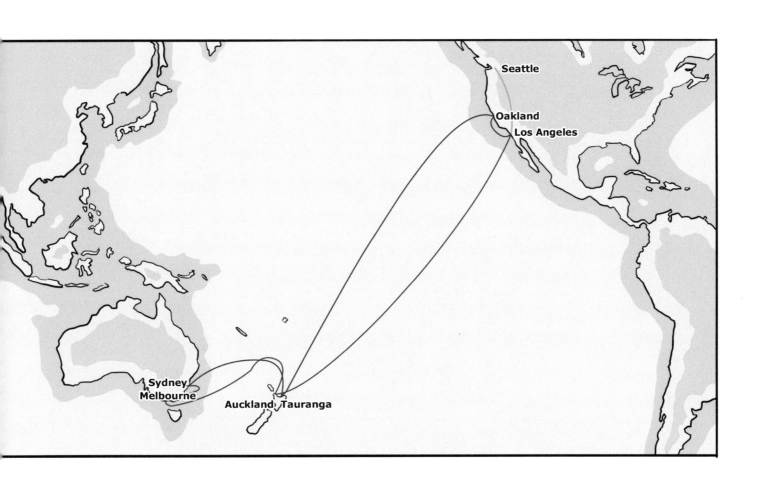

Printed in the United States
by Baker & Taylor Publisher Services